Fears of Your Life

Book Design by Jason whitlow.

Part of "Fears of your Life"
was originally produced as part
of the zine "whipper snapper
Nerd" Published by Harrell Fletcher
and Elizabeth Meyer.

Fears of Your Life

Written and illustrated
by
Michael Bernard Loggins

Manic D Press
San Francisco.

PART ONE

Things that you are very Fearful of

1. Fear of Hospitals and Needles.

2. Fear of school and Dentists.

3. Fear of Black Cats.

4. Fear of Monsters being under my bed. Fear of intruders coming into the house to steal things and hurt us all.

5. Fear of going to jail as being punish for doing something very wrong and have to stay in for a long time.

6. Fear of being Followed.

7. Fear of Dogs.

8. Fear of Strangers.

9. Fear of time Bombs.

10. Fear of Deep waters.

11. Fear of Noises and bumps in the middle of the night.

12. Fear of being chase by bulls.

13. Fear of being Lost.

14. Fear of Elevators.

15. Fear of Doors when they Slams.

16. Fear of Fires and Smokes.

17. Fear of Guns and Knives.

18. Fear of Authority and Punishment.

19. Fear of Toys that comes on by itself without anyone touching it.

20. Fear of someone doing wrong to you and don't want you to do wrong back to them.

21. Fear of spiders and Roaches. and mouse raccoons and Rats too.

22. Fear of getting in deep trouble. or going to get in deep trouble.

23. Fear of being caught with another woman after Cheating on Your wife.

24. Fear of getting run over by a car when not paying attention.

25. Fear of being caught by being with the person that steals.

26. Fear of Bees.

27. Fear of getting left alone.

28. Fear of going to the Doctor.

29. Fear of Riding in deserted Areas when it's dark.

30. Fear of your life being in great Danger and threaten.

31. There's Los Angeles Fears.

32. Oakland Fears.

33. San Francisco Fears.

34. Fear of torados and Thunders, and lightning too.

35. Fear of being in wrong Places at the wrong time.

36. Fear of dropping your Soda as it hit the ground and Fiz on You.

37. Fear of Planes.

38. Fear of insects.

39. Fear of television when you are afraid that it might Blow out all the lights in the house.

40. Fear of getting hit over the head when you carry lots of dough with you or Bucks.

41. Fear OF Getting in trouble by the Law. When you aren't going by rules.

42. Fear OF Death.

43. Fear OF Cemetery as You Drive by There at Night.

44. Fear of Tall Giraffe.

45. Fear of some birds.

46. Fear of Bears.

47. Fear that the television will Explode if you turn it on.

48. Fear of Earthquakes and Volcano's.

49. Fear of a blasted music on the Radio when you are not aware that the Volume is turn up.

50. Fear of being spankin by a Principal when a parent Give an permission.

51. Fear of Sexually Abused.

52. Fear of rolling down Hill Backward.

53. Fear of Bats.

54. Kids Feared that whatever they have done wrong that they afraid of getting Punishment or their Parents will kill them.

55. Fear of Heights.

56. Fear of storms.

57. Fear of being different.

58. Fear of getting Shot.

59. Fear of getting Put out the house.

60. Fear of if I do something naughty I will cause something to happen to me and I will get into trouble.

61. Fear of Rattlesnakes.

62. Fear of Fog Horn.

63. Fear of High tides.

64. Fear of Pirates.

65. Fear of Blackouts.

66. Fear of Disease and Germs.

67. Fear of Hurricanes.

68. Fear of Witches and Gobblins.

69. Fear of Dangerous weApons.

70. Fear of Dragon.

71. Feared that if you get in the way of a Tall tree when it get chop or sawed For it to come tumbling Toward you get out of the way because it liable to Fall on you and kill you and it wouldn't be such a beautiful sight to See.

72. Fear of Firecrackers and cherry bombs. Fire works.

73. Feared wind and Rain Heavy Rain. Hailing Rain.

74. Fear of Police.

75. Fear of scary Ghost stories.

76. Fear of wild Animals.

77. Feared that you will get Scald by a skillet on a stove if it turn over on you. if it get real Hot!

78. Fear of being barefooted walking around the House without any shoes on your Feet Just liable to get tuck on a tack or Glass or Nails or piece of Metal or something.

79. Fear of Nightmare.

80. Fear of hurting themself.

81. Feared of being left in the house alone afraid that there would be an Earth quake in Few more Seconds.

82. Fear that if you are bad or naughty Noone's isn't going to Love You any more.

83. Fear of a Glass table if it cut you.

84. Fear of Dreaming that you have got sunk down into Quick sand.

85. Feared that if you put too much of toilet paper in the toilet Bowl it will run over and get all over the Floor and on you and on someone else too. It would leak From up stairs to the Next Floor Below.

86. Fear of somethings that are Scary.

87. Fear of getting hugged by somebody you don't like is Scary.

88. Fear of stepping down from something that is higher than you thought it was is scary.

89. Fear of Roller skating down Hill when you haven't learned How to stop is scary.

90. Fear of Doing something you shouldn't be doing is scary.

91. Fear of something that you think that could be in the closet that might be scary is scary.

92. Fear of cars when they skid like if you think they're going To crash is scary.

93. Fear of cows and Buffalo's

94. Fear of a dark house.

95. Fear of hearing somebody coming towards the door at midnight.

96. Feared michael heard the cable ·on the 5 Fulton Bus popped like a loud Firecracker it Scared him and the Bus driver Sunday November 11, 1992. At midnight.

97. Fear something is scaring Blackie tonight.

98. People are fearful of me which I wonder is they think that I'm all that terrible or I'm thinking that they think I'm not Human at all Because when they sit next to me than they get back up and move away From me I maybe a stranger But that doesn't make me a Created monster or Something like that. People Aren't Humans they Act like ignorance Dogs with their tail in back of their legs or in Between their middle Bodies their legs. they don't Think who's Feelings they hurt at all they Just do it No Consideration For whatever.

99. People don't think about how they hurt my feelings or don't give a hoot they don't give a crap.

100. Ignorance: No kind of sense at all whatsoever stupid and conceeded and no consideration for me always scared and move away to the next seat from me. People now a days are mean only thinking of themselves noone else.

101. What people think of
     when they see me coming
     up the street?
     What the First thing
     that they can think of
     once they see a stranger
     like me coming in the
     Direction I goes in?
     Nothing But Fear!

102. Why do people when they
     see me coming what do
     they tell their friends?
     let's cross the street I
     don't want to get Hurt.

103. We better cross the
    Street this man is
    Following us and he wants
    To bother us what we
    ought to do is Turn and
    go another Direction
    Fear.

104. what does Fear itself can
    do to make you afraid of
    a stranger and what does
    That Fear tells you about
    that man And what Fear
    Cause you to think something
    may happen to you in just
    5 Seconds or 1 minute?
    Does Fear warns people to
    move away From him or is
    it that it's a warning system
    tells You that man is ready for

104 continued on: An attack you and Harm you or what kind of Danger your life is when you or guys and girls think to do is it lot Threatening or Just a Kind of situation you may Face soon?

105. what is Fear? what does Fear tells you about a Stranger? Does Fear makes you clever or Does it warns you that you and Your Friends Needs to protect yourselves From Danger!

106. Does Fear makes you Smart or Does it Takes you over? It tries But it also Save your life! It helps you To avoid problems and Protect you and Keep you Safe From Harm.

107. I better not stick my Feet out in the side of my bed or the monsters will bite me or wanting to eat me So I better Stay Feet. That's Fear For you!!

108. People that Say that they aren't afraid of anything is ashamed To admit it and they are Just Plain ignorance and just lying to admit that they have as much Fear as the next guy they Know

that they DO Fear Different things
they are lying Because they don't
want anyone to Know how Fearful
they really are.

109. mamma's fearful of michael's
little T.v. is that she's afraid
That it liable to blow out all
the lights in the house. But
I Solve her Fear by showing
her that it works pretty good
now I still don't Know if she
is Fearful or not? Are you?
yes or No circle which
Answer is what you choose
is right.

110. Fear of Ghost stories in the
Dark room.

111. Fear of Boogeyman.

112. Fear of Killer Bees.

113. Fear of Draculars.

114. Fear of Werewolf.

115. Fear of mummy.

116. Fear of widow spider.

117. Fear of Haunted House.

118. Frankenstein is Fearful.

119. Dinosaurs is Fearful.

120. Fear of sharks.

121. Fear of Giantman.

122. Fear of Gorilla.

123. Fear of Godzilla.

124. Fear of Tall woman.

125. Fear of Killer whales.

126. Fear of Dinosaurs bird.

127. Fear of invisiable man.

128. Fear of Blob.

129. Fear of getting molester.

130. Fear of mountain lion.

131. Fear of Apes.

132. Feared when you don't Know that you Feel that somebody liable to Sneak up on you as if you were being surprised. is scary.

133. Fear is like this: someone like a woman that you grab a hold of her hand and going down the escalator when of a sudden you happens to be holding a stranger hand not realizing that she isn't your mother is scary.

134. Fear is like this: If you are ever getting out of your car and not Alert and just going on doing what you normally wouldn't dreamed of doing, not paying Attention and not Thinking clearly or not Focusing on what is happening and not aware or not careful some how ended-up locking your Baby in a closeded in door to your car will have you Panic and it's scary.

135. Fear is like this: Bump in a person that is tall and slim and much older than you standing in line in front of you and you didn't know all that much about him at all you were in Back on him Playing or talking kind of light type tone voice and hetook at you with mean expression on his Face Saying are you talking to me oh No I were thinking about something else. You feel scared Because you think that he thought you were mumbling to yourself in his presence which you thought that you were talking a stranger that isn't your Brother is scary.

136. Staying up late late late at night watching Horror movies alone is scary.

137. Feared that the Bus Driver
is **Driving** much Too Fast
like if He don't know How
to stop it or He tries
slowing it down some so
that he wouldn't Hurt up
Bunch of passengers.
They're scare of his
Driving.

138. Fear of Jumping off
the Bridge way up
High going down real deep
splash in that Deepest
water and take your own
Life away From yourself.
you'll Jump From Top ledge.

Part II

what fears can do to you

Fear # 1.

If you run in the rain, you can slip on a wet pavement which is made out of cement

Equipment also stands For Ground as in Light Gray and Dark Gray as Michael Bernard Loggins Choose to call those Things:

Fear # 2.

I Fear that those tv.
People would take off
my Favorite cartoon.
the Rugrats off the Air
And Wouldn't be able to
Watch Them Anymore For
a long long, long time.
"Please let well enough alone."
Please Don't take my Rugrats
Cartoon off the Air Because
I Love that Cartoon.
Let there Be a Possibility
that Life with the Rugrats
Stays Put means Leave my
Rugrats Cartoon on tv. Michael Said.

Fear # 3.

Want to Know more about
Fears: And what it can
happen to you if you
still be afraid and you
hasn't really truly over
come the Kind of Fear
that you happens to have
on you? You look like
you'll Almost never
get your chance of
over coming it like if
you are Home alone.

Fear # 4.

what will happen if
No one in this Life
inside their community
would ever get over their
Fears of over coming
The fact that they're
really TErrifyed of
Scariest Movies and
Scariest Car Scares Crashes
or Scariest Halloween
Horroriest most Frightened
Holiday seasonal christmas
Time events on T.V. set.
in their Homes:

Fear # 5.

I'm afraid of my Fear of
Crossing the streets of
San Francisco when there
are So much safety rules
of streets For people to
go by the Laws and not
break those safety rules of
Those streets to those whom
Liable to be playing Ball or
Cat and dogs and people may
be Crossing them may Be
Fearing that something alUFul
liable to happen to Some of
Them.

Fear # 6.

Fear that if I go into the Library and I happens to get like 7 or 8 Books and I happens to Find a place in the Library that I would get a lot Comfortable and Begin Reading in those 7 and 8 Books but one Book at a time and I Start to read and (Some How my Voice of mine start to get From low to High and thinking that there weren't anyone Elses) reading theirs and I Look over the People in the Library and I get Fearful and I'll Say OOP's Sorry.

Fear # 7.

Only Dangerous thing about Stop Lights they don't Stay on Long enough For you to Change your mind about Crossing the street. Look Like it Should stay on Like 45 seconds So that you Can go Cross the street. But when they Stay on For 30 seconds They Start to Change Before you get to go across the street. Fear that someday those stoplights going to get You Killed by lots of Charging racing cars Coming your way And that wouldn't be Such a Pretty sight to see if you get my drift sir.

Fear # 8.

One time when Michael Bernard Loggins went out by San Francisco Ocean Beach in California like real Late at Night while the Buses were still running, He saw this Raccoon Diggins in the Garbage can For Food to Eat Michael once Looked over at that Animal and Hurried over on the other side of the street by where the mountain is til He got Fearfully of that Animal and try to go as Far as He can til He's is out of that Raccoons sight where the Raccoon can't see Michael any more, Michael went for the Bus.

Fear # 9.

Fear of Being with a Friend that you have recently met start to take you places with him and you doesn't Know him all that well. You didn't Know that he were gonna bring you Fear and lots of trouble your way. Some one you doesn't Know all that well starts to Carry you in the store to buy you and him something to Eat and Drink and All of a sudden something very fishy starts to Happen; Like For instance your Friend that you are with Could be up to trouble And whoever with him could be heading in For Trouble as well especially if a Friend of yours could be bringing you trouble by stealing a big package of orero cookie.

Fear # 10

I sometimes Fear that
when I walk down our
worses steepest Hill
on our street At olmstead
and Dartmouth I Fear
That some day My Knee
Joint liable to give out
And I wouldn't be able to
walk on my Leg til someone
In my Family rush me up
To the Hospital to Have an
Operation on my Knees
In order to get them to
Work once again, where
they can get back to
walking all over again so
Michael Bernard Loggins
Feel ReFreshed and New Again.

Fear # 11.

Fear of Different kinds of Things.

1. Afraid to be in your bedroom alone.

2. Afraid there's a monster underneath your bed.

3. Afraid to be around Troublemaker people up to No good.

4. Going to Restaurants where you are afraid of people you doesn't know sitting around with a cup with change. And Decide that he wants your money and all of it.

5. What will you do if you were on your own what can you do if something happens would you Panic or Break out into BIG Fear.

Fear # 12.

Fear if you put things
that doesn't Belongs in
Your Ears And You Bust
The Drums Thats are in
Your Ears it Liable to run
You deaf where you can't
Hear anything at all.
You wouldn't be able to Hear
Cars when they're coming at
You. That can be a Frightening
and Very Horrible Situation
to Happen to you If it hada
Occurrance in real Life
especially if You comes
involved in it.
Can You get Hit by cars
If You Can't Hear them.

Fear # 13.

Fear of troublemaker zone
starts with people starting
Trouble on Every single
Transportational like cars
Buses - Trains - streets
- malls - and Banks and Parks,
They May Be all over the
Place.
Fear.
Feel AS Do if You are trap
inside a Fire of a High
UP Floor in a High up Building
Some place in a room and
Can't get out. Call the
Fire Department. It's in
Emergency. A woman or
a child or a Man - or a Boy
is in Some trouble, House on Fire.

Fear # 14

Would you be Fearful
if a rain cloud stodd
over your Head and rain
All over you?

Would you be Fearful if
It Follows You Everywhere
You go And it just Scares
the Heck out of you?

The rain Clouds is so Dark
Gray Weather we have and
It start to Pour like lots of
Buckets of rain water All
over You and You will be
All Drenched   all over
Yourself From The rain
water itself said Michael
Bernard Loggins.

Fear # 15.

Going down the hills on a
Wagon and Don't Know How
to stop it and Feel that
You are going to tip over
On Your Body and Your
Pretty Face And Be hurted
all over and Ache all over
Your whole body would be
a lot Fearfuliness.
And very scary too.

Fear # 16.

I was fear of these two Dogs
That Man had with him when
He was out walking down on
Haight and cole street yesterday
Michael Bernard Loggins has a
Bad case of Anixety and
He's Afraid of those two Pitt
Bulls except my own Dog
Blackie: I Love him said
Michael Bernard Loggins:

Pitt Bulls are very very
Dangerous to us ALL.

Fear # 17.

Have you ever get the
Feeling that if you
go out in the worser
wintertime bad weather
that you Fear that
you just liable to get
the worser wintertime
Cold and have to Stay
in bed lot longer than
you intended to do.?
worser wintery cold
seasonal rest of
the wintertime in
your Bed in the
House.

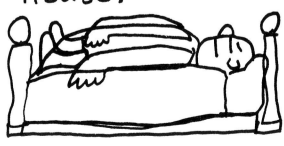

Fear # 18.

When I went out by san Francisco Ocean Beach of Greathighway. These people Were sitting by this one House when I got off the 71 Haight and Noriega Bus To go toward My Brother Darryl and my sister in-Law Simone House Then these people two Dogs Come towards Michael Bernard Loggins like if they want to Attack him. Just because hE Happens to be Let off The Bus on that side of the street like if those Dogs Feel like they own it. Yes. Michael Bernard Loggins Got Fearful and scared Thought those Dogs were gonna Come After him or Chase him.

Fear # 19.

Fearful of using the Bus
that I normally would ride
going home or going for my
Outtings and These Bus Drivers
Drives Pretty crazy and
Very Frightfully that you
have to Grabbs onto Bars
in order to Brace yourself
From Further Accidental
Crash or tip the Bus over
on it's Sides and you Liable
to get seriously hurt or Lucky
to Come out of it Alive or
Die. Now that's the Possibility
That Life is an Sacrafice
That Life Challenge you:

Fear # 20.

I'm Afraid and Fearful
That Pigeons don't know
Right From wrong to not go
out into the street.
They Don't have the kind of
Memory as we humans
does to know what to do
And what shalt Not Do.
They must Don't know the
Danger of their Lives
are Being Jeopardize and
They Must Don't know
What can definitely
happen to them to Human's
Knowledges in sense,
Right Safe Lives and
Danger wrong Lives of theirs.
they Land just Any where
they can Find to Land on surface.

Fear # 21.

Michael is afraid and Frightening and Fearful When Andreascher goes away For a very very, very Long Long, Long, Long Vacational Trips in order To go Traveling all over the world almost like different Places and different Cities and countries to visit People in her own Image and Own Language. He Afraid Andrea scher would come back to San Francisco California with all Different Accents and won't be able to Speak Michael's English or not be able to Understand his words that he's telling her. Like Merry Christmas!

Fear # 22.

I am Afraid Someday I Liable to get lost inside Children's Hospital if I'm not all so familiar with that Place yet. It's going to take some time to get Use to it. Fearfully of that Great big Humungous Children's Hospital There ever would be to Michael's Knowledge. Good that Michael's Sister is Driving him up there on Tuesday January 15, 2002. even though she's with him she Can easily get lost too.

Bad situation to tangled up in. especially if you that Person has an Appointment at 10:45 Am in The morning. Michael Bernard Loggins does.

Fear # 23.

Francis-Michael is Afraid to
To tell you that Christmas
Day is gonna be on a
Wednesday December 25,
2002 this coming year.
And tuesday December 24,
2002 will be totally Different
Than Before. It won't be
Just like Before. I think
Wintertime will be on Sunday
December 22, 2002 winter
Seasonal year that We'll be
having and happens to have.
all at once in a Lifetime
Guaranteed at your bargain
Price just one of michael's
Wintertime humority Funny
Word to Describe his Funny
Humorous Joke Just For the
Laughs of Laughter. by Michael
Bernard Loggins. Keep us Laughing.

Fear#24

Michael is afraid and very
Frightening and Fearful to
Talk all day And Not get
any work done in order
To get some money But
Michael Fear if He Joke around
Too much and doesn't do his
work he wouldn't get any
money at all.
If he Fool around and not
get his work catch up on.

oh! my goodness
is Michael
Really seriously
afraid of that?

Fear # 25.

Fear of People Popping Fire
Crackers and Any Kind of
Dangerous Fire Chemical
Gun Powder around where
Cars are Parked - People
Frightens michael Bernard
Loggins where he sits at
especially be where Cars are
Parked - People Could Put
Michael Bernard Loggins
Life in danger Just being
too carelessness of the
Situation and Don't have
No Care in the world what
so ever if they Act as if
They don't have senses of
5 Just the way God Gave
us to have to use. If in Case
4th of July ever Comes back I
Just Hope it don't be trouble at all.

Fear # 26.

Fear your Life is really
a Challenge and a
Possibility and Choice
and Serious Danger and
warning: and Sacrafice
to Pick: There's Trouble
out into the streets of
San Francisco California
with These Crazier People
Driving Behind these wheels
of these Automobiles
hurting and Hitting People
is Very Frightening And
Very Nerve Wrecking to your
Safety and Life too.

Fear # 27.

Michael Fear that if his teacher Francis Doesn't Put away michael's Top Ramen Noodles UP in The Desk Drawer that Douglas will see it and He'll Liable to want to take it and He'll happens to Eat UP Michael Bernard Loggins' Noodles himself And Michael Bernard Loggins would be out of Luck But He would Have to go Home tonight and Bring Back to School another Pack of Noodles to Eat Himsef So that Wouldn't Ever Ever Happened with that Douglas Eat UP Noodle Story.

Fear # 28.

It's very scary and Fearfully to be sleeping in Your Bed in the middle of the Night whenever There's a Telephone right beside the bed on your Left Near the Door you once Enter and Exit out. You are sleeping The Telephone rang and scare the Living Life out of you, in the middle of the Night. "Who is this calling at this Hour of Night?

Fear # 29.

I would be Afraid if a Car Somewhere Almost close. And it was going to Explode I would run as Fast as I Can to get out of the way of it So That I wouldn't get Hurt by it. I'll get away as Far as I can or Hit the Deck Means to Drop Down and wish it don't get you It's a Car Exploding, It's a Scary Situation For you to See would it ever occur For Real or does it Happen So Other, or what Happens after a Car are through Exploding will the Fire Fighter's Puts The Fire out?

Fear # 30.

There's a possibility
That something fearful
and very Scary
Liable to Happen
which is a warning
Sign that you can't
Understand what it
means can Scare the
Heck out of you.

Fear # 31

Watch a Fearful Movie at Night
Late and when you go to bed
to sleep then All of a sudden
The Nightmare start to
Happen And You start to
Break a sweat From having
an Anxiety Depression
Scariness and Fearful Night-
Mare Pictures in your Mind.

Nightmare is a Dream
that frightens People.

Freddie Kruger Don't exist
in the real Life, the world
only in Movies - Nightmare
on Elm Street, The Fiction
Stories on But Never REAL
LiFE.

Fear # 32.

Fear of People up to No
Good Making Trouble in
our Community and
Schools and in our

Neighborhoods And our
Cities too:

" streets of Trouble
maker Hood."

Fear # 33.

Fear of you Never Known you were gonna lose your Mother is very Sad and scary Experience you have to Face and learn From and You wonder why she has to die I Love her- And I had Loved her once while she were Alive.

especially if she was the mother that raised you and the others through Birth And You only wish that you could have done all you can to Help Save her Life.

It Gonna be a worse times and hard times For Michael BernardLoggins and his Sisters and Brothers too. especially when Mother's Day comes.

Fear # 34.

If your friends are people that you are with and you Hear them making Decision about what they DEcide That they are gonna Steal expensive and very valuable merchanoise out of the Department stores and don't careless. You Say I'm out of hEre! Bye-bye. I'm not getting caught in your crazy schemes. I'm Not Your Stealer Partner, zim just your Friend. it's gonna trouble And it's on your head not mine. I'm not gonna Participate in stealing with You. So Leave me out out of Your crazy schemes especially If it involves orero cookies and other stuff, Hot stuff. Fear of me getting In trouble Just as well.

Fear # 35

I Fear that in the story of Little Red riding Hood the Girl goes out in the woods by herself (without Anyone else going too) to her Grandmothers House so that she wouldn't Just get suspicious that something Liable to Happen to the Girl all in the woods alone trying to get to her Grandmothers House And Delivers a Basket of Goodies to her Grandmother and What happen is that her Grandmother turns out to be the Mean and Worser wolf around- want to Eat up the Girl it's ownself.

Fear # 36.

Life can be very challege.
When it comes to Danger
and Crossing the streets of
San Francisco and other streets
And other parts of the world
especially in other Neighborhoods
Is where Fear Lurkes out For
You in Some way.
Bring you lots of Fears and
Trauma in Your Hands Feets
and Body.
Bring you shakes and Trembles
To you.

Fear # 37.

Grabbing onto someone elses
Grandmother which you thought
she were yours And you
haven't ever thought that
Those Grandmother's that
you haven't seen that has
Passaway from what your
Parents has told you that
your Grandparents Has
Passaway Before you were
Born is scary and Fearful
Situation to be in.
yes. it Can Happen by
Accident.

Fear # 38

Walking into a lion's cage
and petting it on the head
can be a Ticklish situation,
and not in a funny way.

Fear # 39.

I would be very fearful if
I reached up on top shelf
Trying to Reach for a nice
Thicker covered Dictionary
Book And not ask for Help
From Someone and the Books
Come off the shelf and
Make lots of noises and
the people gets Angry at
me and Don't understand that
I had want Help But I were
Afraid to ask for it and they
be a Jerk or a creep as
Hope tells me and People
Say that I'll have to Pay For
the Shelf and I get in lots of
Trouble behind it. Says Michael.

Fear # 40.

Fear of streets in our
Cities and Communities
and Neighborhoods are
very rare Sometimes
People are very Carelessly
designated drivers unImpatience
Not Given You any time what so ever
Crossing the streets of San Franc
isco, Making it or Cities in the
world a lot unSafe For Children
Adults and Animals to Cross them
and Makes us Paralyzed From
the waist on down to Your Feet.
How dangerous Streets really
are These days in our Lives:

Fear # 41.

Michael Bernard Loggins
have to Move the Noodle
Bowl with the Noodles in it
over So he wouldn't Knock
it off the table and Bust
the Bowl open into Pieces
And Noodles all over the
Creativity Explored center
Floor, I Feared it Liable
to Happen that way,
So that's Why I Kinda
Shoved the Bowl over in
the Middle of my table
to Prevent it From
Happening to it Breaking
to Pieces or in Half too.

Fear#42.

I Fear that when I'm
going across the Street
on Folsom and 16th I
FEAR that these people
in these cars is going to
Seriously hurt me or
really take my Life
For sure definitely
The way they act
Foolishly and Very
Dangerously with their
Bad worsest Driving
Uneducational Skill
Don't Need Any License to
Be Handled any vEhicles.

Fear # 43

Fear And Traumatized
Frightful Experience of
Your Life Michael
Bernard Loggins Books
He was making as All
Stories that He invented
on his own in his head.
Thoughts coming out
like left and right.
Didn't Know How Fast they
was coming at me., It's
like Somebody were get
ready to throw a Fast
Ball at the Base Ball Game.
Says michael Bernard Loggins.

Fear # 44.

Two Fear of my hand is Hurting and why is it Hurting when I'm writing according on how hard I'm Holding my Pen And If it keep on Hurting it liable to Hurt a lot worser Than Now; Says "michael Bernard Loggins."

Fear # 45

Afraid this is the Last
Thing that ever occur
to me. this is the End
of Fears of your Life
Page in my Book.
Tuesday February 19,
2002. is when michael
Bernard Loggins Finishes
These Pages up. so there
be the Last to be done.
For michael Bernard
Loggins. Congradulation!
michael My Buddy Buddy!
Pal you Did it you got it done.

Michael Bernard Loggins was born in 1961 in San Francisco, California.

He has been writing, drawing and painting at Creativity Explored since it's inception in 1984. His words and Art have been exhibited at galleries in San Francisco, Los Angeles and New York.

Michael has a sizable collection of 45's (somewhere in the neighborhood of 500-600 discs) and sings on occasion. He has a cassette tape of songs he has sung while accompanying himself on the coffee can.

His list of Fears have been enjoyed by a growing list of admirers and have been exhibited at the Yerba Buena Center For the Arts, Published in the Sun and Harper' Magazine, and read on NPR's This American Life.

Currently michael is most interesting in writing and this usually takes the Form of notes to Friends, issues on his Mind (safety, allergies, emotions etc.) and recounting incidents From his Life. His Drawings Generally deal with lighter subJect matter such as animals, Idyllic worlds and Imaginary People.

He likes spending time at ocean Beach and the panHandle near Golden Gate park in San Francisco. He Frequently takes himself out to lunch and enjoys hangout at his girlfriend Hope's House till 8:30 P.M.

" THE thank you Note to people that I know in my Life. throughout my Life." "That's the titled."

1. I want to thank Francis For helping me with my Fears of your life Book by helping me to get it Finish and ready to have it Publighed and ready to Be made. Michael and Francis Are doing the work together.

2. I want to thank my Girlfriend Hope Goodall For being my Girlfriend All the way up to 12 years of being together in a long 12 years relationship with me And Say that You Love me a whole lot and I Love You too. and you go Places with me and You treat me to Lunch Just the way I treated you Hope Darling Baby, you are my Love in this 12 year Relationship. From Friday August 2, 1991 you are the best.

3. thank you Erika Lee Altman and Katie Wyatt For Coming to creativity Explored Center 2 Art day Program to visit me and Hangout with me and most of all thank you both For taking me out to Lunch on You Guys spare time because we haven't got that Chance to do that in our lives till yesterday which was Thursday August 14th 2003. of a Hot and Breezy summer time mix weather we Are having in August 2003. I want to thank my Mother For Everything you done.

4, thank you Todd For taking me out Places
with you and Francis whenever I asked you guys
Nicely. And sorry I didn't get a way of Crossing
the Street of Mission and 16th on wednesday
August 13, 2003. And I couldn't get a chance
to Catch UP to you and Francis by the time
you both got on the 49 mission and City College
bus wednesday And the worse Part way I couldn't
Catch up to you and Francis at all. Not only
that: My Foot Start to hurt me real badly
And I was in Pain For a little While And I
have came From Walgreens and Rode this other
49, mission and City College Bus And still I couldn't
Catch up to you Guys For Nothing in the world!
And the only thing that happened to me is on
Vanness and Market street the Bus
Driver on the 71 Haight and Noriega Bus took
off and left me behind him and didn't give me
Anytime to get on the Bus And that's When
I got Furious at him. He was too Impatient
didn't have time to Wait for me what so ever.
So my Foot begin to Hurt me instead.
Says Michael Bernard Loggins, I went straight
To Jack's Record cellar.

Life will be at creativity Explored no matter
what the circumstances will be.
Whether it's good-bad-or worse than what it
seems or even those things kind of get wacky,
or slightly out of hand, soon or Later, These
things blows over and return to what
they will be.

– Michael Bernard Loggins.